The dark rose

Denise Soules

Presentation by *BookLeaf Publishing*

Web: www.bookleafpub.com

E-mail: info@bookleafpub.com

ISBN: 9789358314120

First edition 2023

DEDICATION

I dedicate this book to all who read it, may your journey be smooth, and the destination worth the struggle.

I also dedicate this book to my children, may you never give up on your dreams, and always rise from the darkness.

ACKNOWLEDGEMENT

I want to acknowledge the many people I've lost along the way, if it wasn't for your spirit, love, and support, I would never have had the strength to carry on. Your lives were cut short, but the memories I have, will live on as long as I have breath to breathe.

PREFACE

Poetry is thought to be cutesy, and rhythmic, but it's so much more than that. Poetry has the power to inspire, to engage readers, and to captivate the mind. It is my hope readers will question the depths of my soul and create a visions, they themselves can identify with.

The Fall

Young love, rare and exquisite.
Each moment is better than the last.
Each day somehow brighter.
Two souls merging as one.
A love strong as the sun.
All is well, all is well.

Suddenly the souls are ripped apart.
Death comes, and shatters one heart.
Darkness sweeps in, and the tears pour down.
Suddenly no peace, to be found.
All is not well, not well at all.

Years pass, the memories they made.
Slowly, and surely begin to fade.
With time you will heal, the people say.
The pain reduces, day by day.
One step closer to the end.
When one heart,will be two again.
The sun rises another day.
All is well, all is well.

The clouds roll in, and out like the ocean.
The tides, nothing, but raw emotion.
Once a love like this is lost.

It can never, truly be found again.
All is not well, not well at all.
For this is the reason, the reason for the fall.

Frozen in time.

Your eyes are captivating, they seep into my
soul, ravage my thoughts, know every struggle,
and see every tear.
Nothing around me matters because I am frozen
in time.

My hand reaches for yours, the energy is
electric, it makes my skin tingle.
You restore my faith, and charge my heart like
an engine charges a battery.
With each beat, I feel, I'm frozen in time.

Should I wither away, and my body be turned to
ash.
You will be there always holding me, we are
side by side, ever ready to take on the world.
I won't feel you though, because I'm frozen in
time.

Your lips touch mine and our universe implodes.
Your like the fuse that sets off a nuclear reaction
inside my soul.
But no one sees us because we are frozen in
time.

We are everywhere, and nowhere, all at once.
We are one body, mind, and soul.
Connected by this fabric of time.
We are inhaling one another's aura, and time no
longer, can hold us.

It all comes together.

Lies kill the soul you tell.
Pain doesn't really exist.
Love breaks the heart.
Hope leaves you hopeless.
Sorrow makes you remember.
Death forces you to live.
Happiness creates sadness.
Excitement leads to downfall.
Downfall builds you up.
When your up, the only place to go is down.
Joy leads to disappointment.
Disappointment brings you courage.
Courage brings frustration.
Frustration leads to a solution.
Solutions create new problems.
Problems cause confusion.
Confusion illuminates your path
Paths are meant to be traveled.
Traveling leaves you grounded.
Grounding causes chaos for everyone.
Everyone isn't any one.
Only you, are a part of me.

Lost Whispers

The moon illuminates the darkness.
Shadows fall.
We really aren't alone at all.
The owl hoots, the wolf howls.
Two hearts can't wait, until tomorrow.
A gentle touch, a hurried kiss.
We run off, into the dark abyss.
Ever so softly, I hear a whisper.
Good night my love, goodnight.

Death

Paralyzing devastation.
All across this once great nation.
Mother's, fathers, husbands, wives.
Death affects all their lives.
Cannot see an end in sight,
What a sad pathetic plight.
Please don't leave me, don't let up.
Sorry dear I can't get up.
My chest is heavy, my breath is weak.
Death is only for the meak.
All around you see them suffer.
Crying, screaming, for their mother's.
Mom is not there, not here this night.
For she lost the battle, she lost her life.

Hands

The river flows triumphantly through the land.
It is here, where you grab my hand.
We walk through the dense evergreen trees.
Enjoying the ever gentle breeze.

I close my eyes, and breathe in deep.
For this moment, I wish to keep.
Your face is branded into my mind.
As I slowly, fall behind.
I move swiftly, to match your pace.
So that I can feel, your soft embrace.
Your hand slowly caresses my side.
For once, I don't feel like, I must hide.
You pull me close, I lift my chin.
Our lips meet, once again.

The power of love, flows through my soul.
My heart is, suddenly, quite full.
The river flows through the land, and it all
started with the touch of your hand.

My Son

The excitement I felt, when they told me, that
day.
I never thought, would go away.
It was a warm dreary spring morn, when they
told me, when you would be born.
"Tragic some would mutter," others, "such a
shame. "
I couldn't bring myself, to even say your name.
Your heartbeat once, made the quaintest sound.
It could still be heard, from miles around.
The doctor told me come in, that day.
That day my son, you passed away.
The doctor asked, "what should we do?"
"Should we save him, or should we save you?"
"Save my child please," I said.
The doctor tried, untill he turned red.
Then he said to me, "my lady, it is time now to
hold your baby.
If I keep trying to make him survive,
you will never see him alive.
Hold him now, and enjoy his smile.
You only have, but a short while."
I held you close , and gazed deeply into your
eyes.

Your breaths show a decline, as I watched your
demise.
Death shall swallow us up together,
That I will never forget, not ever.

Simple Things

The morning dew,
The smell of rain.
The evening hues,
Of summers gain.

The fresh cut grass,
The smell of smoke.
A crystal glass,
The funny joke.

A single tear
A winding creek.
It's all made clear,
At the end of the week.

A summer love,
Drifted away.
The sky above,
Turns quite gray.

Alas the fall,
And all the glory.
Begin the crawl,
And do not worry.

For life is this,
As simple as it may be.
A lovers kiss,
A hope for eternity.

Thankful

In life, there is what is, and what will be.
In death there is what was, and what came to
thee.
In love, there are the memories, and great
moments.
In hate, there is the anger, and disappointment.
In happiness there is joy, and hope.
In sadness there is fear, and learning to cope.
So many feelings for us to have, and share.
For that, I am thankful to have someone there.

Untouchable

If I were a bird, I would tweet and fly,
Above the mountains, and all the trees.
You could never catch me, for I would be
untouchable.

If I were a wolf, as fierce as night.
With my sharp teeth, and piercing eyes.
You could never catch me for I would be
untouchable.

If I were a butterfly, gentle, and at peace.
I'd float around, through the flowers, and the
rocky seas.
You could never catch me for I would be
untouchable.

I am me, not perfect, or pretty.
But I am; as free as a bird, as fierce as a wolf,
and as gentle as a butterfly.
You can catch a glimpse of me, but my dear,
please never forget, I am untouchable.

I am

I can do all things I must do, but not all of them, can I do without you.
I will make sure each day I try, and trying I'm told, is half the battle.
I am never going to look back, because nothing in my future, is from my past.

I can see our future, and know it is our past, that melds us together.
I will always be honest, loyal, and true, to your heart.
I am falling in love with the person you are, but also who you aspire to be.

I can give you love, and also respect your boundaries.
I will never let us go to bed angry, or upset.
I am the one person, who truly understands your pain.

I can love you, through your pain, and also your journey.
I will never leave your side, where we go, we go together.

I am certain that you are the one person, I need
in my life.

I can give you the space you need, to become
better.
I will not forget you, but love you from afar, and
always be with you, in your heart.
I am willing to walk through the mud, and the
muck, to get us to paradise.

I can tell you, I am in love with you.
I will always be careful with your heart, and
never intentionally hurt you.
I am here, I am me, I am real, and I am yours, if
you want me.

Leaves

Your intricate lines, and detailed shapes.
Your chameleon ability, to adapt to seasons.
The feel of you on my skin, soft, yet spikey.
Your cycle of life is short, and yet eternal.
You may float on the water, or sink to the
bottom.
You can be soft, or crunchy.
You are one thing, and yet it takes thousands of
you, to make one whole.
You are simple, and yet so complex.
The sun wakes you up.
The evening makes you wither.
You are the mighty leaf.

Weathered Leather

Just when you think you have it all figured out.
When, it all seems to come together.
This is when you learn what life is about.
When life, throws you leather.

It's hard, and easy, at the same time.
Nothing you do, seems to make it any better.
When the day is almost done, and you think
you've surely won.
Only to find your running out of leather.

If you allow yourself the time to rest, you've
already lost.
If your fortunate enough, to never ever lose.
Don't contemplate your thoughts.
No this is not a ruse.

One day you'll wake to find, your life has passed
you by.
And all that you've been left with, is leather
that's run dry.

Love Burns

The love of a lifetime,
Lives within your soul.
If you do not kindle it,
the fire cannot grow.

Some people try to smother it,
The fire slowly dies.
Yet people forget,
Love cannot grow through lies.

To love another person,
Your selfishness must end.
If it does not, love will surely bend.

Love is a fickle thing,
Bending leads to break.
Even hearts mingling.
Cannot claim a stake.

Even the greatest fire,
Needs oxygen to thrive.
Love is not any different,
It needs fire to stay alive.

Pain

Pain, a simple word, that simply means, so
much. Physical pain, can be caused by just a
simple touch.

Emotional pain is different, no marks can be
seen.
But in your mind, and in your soul
its the deepest, darkest, dream.

Emotional pain is clever
when you have, turned your back.
It crawls up in your warped mind,
and just gives you a smack.

Verbal pain the words you can't escape.
Once the words were uttered, you knew they
were a mistake.

To late to take them back now, no apology will
do. Nothing hurts worse, than the pain that's
caused by you.

Should I, could I, no.

21

I don't want to lose you, because I did not say.
The words I should've said to you, before you
went away.

Could I have changed our start, by letting you
within my heart.

I suppose this I'll never know, because I let you
go.

The Rocky Way

My path was not a path at all, but a bunch of
jagged rocks.
My feet ached from all the miles, that I had on
lock.
Sadly, my mind was worse for wear, and
becoming, quite unraveled.
This is just how it gets, when you take the way
less traveled.

The sky not bright, but weary grey.
The trees around me, had withered all away.
Even the ground beneath my feet, did not feel
very soft. Again, I suppose that's what you get,
when you choose the path of rocks.

Looking all around, to see if I can find,
Something full of beauty, to entertain my mind.
I shift my gaze upon the sun, that was a mistake!
Now I'm surely blind, and my skin is getting
baked!

My body is now shaking, my legs feel like
flambe. I guess I should have stayed at home,
this dreary summer day.

Just a few more steps, to get me to the top.
Why did I do this, on this path of rocks? No time
to second guess the motive, or contemplate my
mistakes. I guess this path wasn't so bad, if it
wasn't for the snakes.

Time

Time tics by,
Day and night.
Every day faster than the one prior.
With each passing day,
Your hair begins to gray.
Each moment, creates a new desire.
Your body slows.
It shows.
Suddenly the clock, doesn't tic.
Your life is finished, that's it.
What will the people recall?
How you lived?
Did you live at all?
The clock on the wall ticked through it all.

Lost control

I thought you were the one.
You were nothing, like you showed.
You were a monster, trying to control.
You got inside my head,
Made me feel weak,
Practically dead.
Untill the day I realized,
I didn't need you anymore.
Not to tear me down,
Or throw me on the floor.
Suddenly I was stronger.
I was able to break free.
After all these years i'm finally able, to be me.
The best part,
I'm in control of my heart.
I don't feel lost, or scared, anymore,
You are no longer darkening my door.
I wish you well, and hope you see.
You had it all, then you lost me.
Now that I am free,
One thing I will never be.
In love with anyone,
who wants to control me.

Clarity

Standing on this dock beside the ocean.
My heart is overjoyed and full of emotion.
The waves crash in and out again,

The Beginning of THE END.

Is this the end, or merely the beginning.
Hard to know, when your mind doesn't stop
spinning.
Every day feels like a blur,
Something's missing but your never sure.

Hand in hand we walk in stride.
So glad your here by my side.
Everyone has demons they must face.
Life is truly like a race.

One step forward, two steps back.
Mentally you want to crack.
Just hold on, a little longer.
What doesn't kill you, makes you stronger.

Don't give up, don't give in.
This is the world, we living.
Bending untill, you just might break.
Forget it all, for heaven sake.

You got this, the people say.
But your not sure, everyday.
Don't second guess yourself,
Dive right in.

The time is now let's begin.

Live your life, and just be free.
Love yourself, for eternity.
Put on a smile, and straighten your crown.
Don't let anyone bring you down.

So this is it, this is the end.
Or is it?
Let's being again.

* 9 7 8 9 3 5 8 3 1 4 1 2 0 *